Box Turtle Care

The Complete Guide to Caring for and Keeping Box Turtles as Pets

Pet Care Expert

Copyright © 2015 SouthShore Publications

All rights reserved.

Although the author and publisher have made every effort to ensure that the information in this book was correct at press time, the author and publisher do not assume and hereby disclaim any liability to any party for any loss, damage, or disruption caused by errors or omissions, whether such errors or omissions result from negligence, accident, or any other cause.

ISBN-13: 978-1517152864

ISBN-10: 1517152860

CONTENTS

Introduction 9

Box Turtles as Pets 12
    Buying a Box Turtle 12
    How Many Should You Keep? 14

Box Turtles in the Wild 16
    Natural Habitat 16
    Characteristics 16
    Lifespan 17
    Self-Defense 17
    Diet 18

Housing, Heating and Lighting 20
    Inside or Outside? 20
    Enclosures 20
    Outdoor Enclosures 21
    Indoor Terrariums 23
    Humidity 23
    Substrate 24
    Hides 25
    Plants 25

Water 26

Lighting and Heating 27

Monitoring 29

Feeding and Diet 31

Insects 31

Vegetables, Salad and Fruits 32

How Much Should You Feed? 33

Supplements 33

A Note on Outdoor Enclosures 34

Fasting 35

Breeding 37

Sexing 37

Breeding Conditions 37

Mating Rituals and Process 37

Eggs 38

Hatchling Care 39

Hibernation 42

Diseases and Illness 44

Environment 44

Wild Food 45

Swollen and Closed Eyes 45

    Ear Abscesses 45

    Pneumonia 46

    Sore Skin 46

    Parasites 46

    Things to Look Out For 47

    Choosing a Vet 47

Final Thoughts 49

INTRODUCTION

At Pet Care Expert, we had a very simple idea about how to create the best possible pet care books around. We don't just give you one person's opinion or have 1 person write our books. We had the simple thought that the best way to provide our readers with the absolute best advice on caring for any animal is to put together the collective knowledge of animal experts from all around the world, so that's exactly what we did!

With every book we write on each and every animal, we consult with experts on that particular animal or species from all around the world. The people who advise us and provide us with this valuable information range from everyday people who have had many years of experience keeping the animal in question right through to professionals such as zoo keepers and veterinarians.

This enables us to provide the highest quality information possible and ensure that our books are packed with invaluable content for our readers to enjoy. We don't just cover the basics and essentials either, we specifically ask for "top tips" from our experts, providing a range handy tips and tricks that we throw in throughout the course of the book.

So when reading any of our guides, you can be sure that the advice contained within is 100% accurate and tried and tested by some of the top experts from all around the world. This makes for the happiest healthiest pets around, which in turn makes for the happiest owners and the most enjoyable experience with your new pet.

We also know that you're excited to get start with your new pet and get the knowledge you need to look after them as best as possible in a quick and easy way. So we keep the length of our books down, keeping the information as concise and easy to consume as possible without all of the fluff and pointless information that you don't need. This makes for short, easy to read books that can be enjoyed by everyone, whether you like reading or not.

We have also made things easy for you by including helpful links to products throughout this book so, if your device allows, you can simply click to view the products that our experts have recommended.

So, now you know who we are and what we do, let's get on with the rest of the book. Enjoy!

BOX TURTLES AS PETS

Box turtles have become popular as pets in recent years, as they are very rewarding animals to keep with bags of character.

The needs of box turtles in captivity are hard to meet if you are uneducated on their exact requirements, so it's vital to do your research properly before getting one.

Box turtles don't tend to make great pets for young children. This is mainly because they are prone to stress from over handling and any kind of rough treatment, preferring to live a quiet, relaxed life.

Box turtles can bite, but it's not very common. They only do this when very stressed or, if you feed them with your hands as some people like to do, they may start to associate your fingers with food and try to nip you.

Other than that, they make fantastic pets and keeping box turtles can be a very rewarding experience. As long as you're the type of person who likes to mainly observe your pets rather than interact with them regularly and play with them, owning a box turtle is likely to be ideal for you.

Buying a Box Turtle

Some box turtles are highly stressed by being taken from their homes and moved to a new area. Three toed box turtles don't seem to mind this movement and relocation as much, so we would highly recommend taking a look at them when deciding what variety to keep as a pet, especially for beginners.

Always check where the turtles you are buying have come from. We only recommend buying captive bred box turtles. This is not only much more humane, as taking a wild turtle from its home and putting it in a cage is not really very ethical, but it will also help to stop the wild populations from being diminished.

This is a real problem. It's estimated that numbers into the hundreds of thousands of wild turtles are taken from the wild every year and sold into the pet trade. Many are then kept in terrible conditions until they are resold, with up to half dying before making it to the stores. Even then, these wild caught turtles that you will be buying are likely to be suffering from malnutrition and high stress levels. So really do your research on the person or store you are buying from before making your purchase to ensure you get a healthy turtles and to help stamp out this cruel trade.

Many pet stores will buy almost exclusively wild caught box turtles, so we would suggest that you steer clear of them all together. Instead, check with your local turtle rescue group or reptile society as they will usually have plenty of animals that need a good home. If this option is not available to you, you can always search online for a reputable breeder who is selling their own turtles offspring.

How Many Should You Keep?

Box turtles are certainly an animal that enjoys company. In our experience they are much happier and more likely to do well when kept in a small group.

Overstocking and overcrowding, as with all animals in captivity is always going to be an issue, but if you are keeping your turtles in an outdoor enclosure as we highly recommend (for reasons we will go into later in the book) you should have plenty of space to keep a good number of turtles together.

To give you a rough guideline, a 6ft x 6ft outdoor enclosure can comfortably home around 4 adult box turtles.

BOX TURTLES IN THE WILD

Box turtles are part of the "Terrapene" genus and are members of the American pond turtle family or "Emydidae".

Natural Habitat

Box Turtles are native to North America and Mexico and can be found in a wide variety of habitats throughout these regions. This means that there's not any one strict habitat that is ideal for box turtles. It depends on the exact species.

The most common habitat for box turtles however is a mesic woodland type of environment. This basically means a humid, moisture rich, woodland environment. There are a couple of other types of box turtle that live in much more dry, arid areas such as grassland and almost desert-like regions. There are even some very specific species like the Coahuilan that lives in a relatively small area of marshland. This means that you're going to have to find out the type of habitat that best suits the type of box turtle that you want to keep, before setting up the enclosure.

Characteristics

Box turtles can completely retract inside their shell and tightly seal the gap between their carapace (upper shell) and plastron (underbody) making them very well armored and prepared to defend themselves against predators.

Lifespan

The lifespan of a box turtle in captivity is generally about 50 years, making them one of the longest living pets out there. This means that you should very carefully consider the choice to get one as you will be responsible for these animals for a very long time if they do make it to this age.

Some box turtles can even live up to 100 years if kept and cared for properly throughout their lives. So a box turtle could well be a lifelong commitment.

Self-Defense

Apart from their ability to completely enclose themselves inside their shell, box turtles have a couple of other ways of defending themselves against predators.

The most obvious way is by simply hiding. Box turtles like to be able to hide away if they feel stressed or threatened, so this is something that should always be an option for them inside their enclosure. The other main form of self-defense is biting.

In the wild, the box turtles main predators are animals like raccoons, dogs, skunks and rodents. They are also prey for some birds and even snakes.

Diet

Box turtles and omnivorous animals and they aren't too fussy what they eat really. Their natural diet would include slugs, snails, insects, berries, fungi, worms, roots, flowers, fish, frogs, eggs and much more.

When they are young (under 6 years old) they will tend to eat insects as they are high in protein and therefore provide them with the nutrients that they need to grow and develop. The types of insects that they eat in the wild will vary wildly depending on what they come across, it could be anything from a worm one day to a millipede the next.

As box turtles reach adulthood, they will start eating more greens and fruits as the need for protein for growth diminishes. As adults, box turtles can consume an almost completely vegetarian diet and be perfectly healthy.

HOUSING, HEATING AND LIGHTING

In this section we will discuss keeping box turtles indoors and outdoors and the importance that this holds. We will also discuss the vivarium, or enclosure, that you will be using to keep your turtles. If you haven't heard of a vivarium before, it's just a word used to describe an enclosed area that is used to simulate a natural habitat. Even an aquarium could be described as a vivarium for example, but of course in this instance, we will be trying to simulate the habitat of the box turtle.

Inside or Outside?

Box turtles do need an outdoor enclosure to be as healthy as possible, we would say this is a must. They can be kept inside overnight and let out into an outdoor run every day but this is not ideal as this will cause unnecessary stress. Box turtles like to live in one place and not be moved about. They also need exposure to the sun every day. So it's very important that they are allowed to be outdoors.

If you have no other choice and you have to keep your box turtles indoors then you can still do this, although we do not recommend it. The best choice is a permanent outdoor space with plenty of room for the turtles to explore and roam.

Enclosures

Choosing the size of your enclosure is very important. Many people will start off with something small and choose to upgrade at a later date. In our opinion, you should start off with an enclosure big enough to sustain the box turtle with plenty of room for it to explore for its whole life.

By choosing a large enough enclosure to begin with, you minimize stress and making the turtle feel like it has been uprooted from its home when you decide to switch to a new enclosure.

So get things right the first time round and don't be tempted to rush and get the easiest or cheapest option available. After all, setting up the enclosure and getting everything ready is one of the most fun parts of getting a new pet. So take your time, get everything perfect and ready for your turtle to settle right in and enjoy right away.

So to begin with you will need to select the design and size of your vivarium.

Outdoor Enclosures

One of the best things about outdoor enclosures are that they are much easier to set up and maintain than indoor vivarium. You don't need any artificial lighting or heating and your turtles will be much happier and healthier in a more natural, outdoor environment. Your turtles will also be able to hunt the insects that will inevitably venture inside, which they do very enthusiastically!

Firstly you need to choose your location. A shady spot is ideal as you don't want your turtles to be over exposed to excessive heat at any point as this can lead to health issues. Having said this, turtles do like to bask and they do need sunlight to maintain optimal health. They also need sunlight, especially on cold days, to get their body temperature up. So if you can find an area that gets a couple of hours of direct sunlight in the morning, this would be a perfect location to set up your outdoor enclosure.

As for size, we would recommend a 6 foot run as a great size for box turtles. You could go slightly smaller if you are housing just a couple of turtles and, of course, if you want to go bigger then this will just give your turtles even more room to roam and explore which is going to add to their quality of life and make them even happier. The bigger the better really. Obviously if you are planning on having or breeding quite a few turtles then it's a good idea to have a very large enclosure.

The main concern for anyone keeping turtles in an outdoor enclosure should be security. This is because you obviously don't want your precious turtles escaping, but more importantly, you don't want any predators to get in and try to kill them.

This may surprise some of you, but box turtles are fantastic diggers, which makes them pretty good at escaping the confines of their enclosure. Even if they weren't, you don't want any animals to burrow their way in. The easiest way to help prevent this from happening is to dig a trench where the edges of the enclosure will be and insert a layer of wire mesh underground. Then when you lay the enclosure on top, you can fix the underground wire to the frame and fill the trench back up. This mesh should be at least 12 inches deep underground to make things reasonably safe, although the deeper the better.

The last thing you need to consider is having an area to keep them warm in the colder months. We would recommend covering the enclosure mainly in mesh, but also having some kind of inner enclosed area or having one end of the enclosure cladded in wood or plastic to keep out the wind and to help retain heat.

Indoor Terrariums

There may be circumstances where you need to keep your box turtle indoors. For example, if you have a weak, underweight or sick turtle, you should bring it inside in the colder months as it may not survive hibernation. Or maybe you live in a region where the climate is simply not suitable for keeping turtles outside.

So even if you are intending to keep your box turtles outside for the most part, it's a good idea to have an indoor terrarium set up and ready to go if the need arises. For a single box turtle, you should be aiming for a 30 gallon tank as a minimum.

Humidity

It's important to have a good level of humidity in the vivarium or enclosure when keeping box turtles A general humidity level of about 80% above the surface of the substrate is recommended. To maintain the humidity levels of an indoor vivarium you will need a spray bottle.

We would highly recommend getting a new, unused spray bottle rather than washing one out and reusing it. This is because, although it may look clean and have been thoroughly washed out, it may still contain traces of chemicals that you don't want coming into contact with your turtles.

Brand new spray bottles are very cheap, you can find them at most dollar stores for example. It's best to look for one that has a fine mist setting or to buy a specialist reptile spray bottle. Something like the Exo Terra Mini Mister would be perfect for most applications.

For outdoor enclosures, the rain and dew should do a pretty good job of maintaining humidity. However, if it's particularly hot where you are, or if the rain fall hasn't as heavy as usual, you can simply water the ground in the enclosure along with the rest of your garden.

Substrate

For outdoor enclosures, this is pretty easy. Just earth, grass, weeds and leaf litter is absolutely fine and will simulate a natural habitat very well.

In an indoor vivarium, you have some commercial options that make great choices. Eco Earth Coconut Fiber is fantastic for box turtles and so is Forest Floor Bedding. A mix of these, which should be about 6 inches deep to allow your turtles to dig (4 inches at a minimum), would be absolutely ideal. Then add some Sphagnum Moss for a good humidity maintaining substrate.

Hides

You will need to have two hides in your enclosure. This will give them somewhere to hide, sleep, keep out of the heat and relax. Without any hides, your turtles can feel very exposed and stressed, making for extremely unhappy pets.

It's important to keep in mind how big your box turtles will grow when choosing a hide. For an indoor vivarium, we would recommend the Extra Large Zoo Med Habba Hut as its large enough for most box turtles.

For outdoor enclosures, you can use similar items or you can opt for some kind of pottery drainpipe, pieces of wood, hollowed out logs, etc.

Plants

It's a great idea to have some real, natural plants in your vivarium to provide that natural habitat feel for your turtles. Nothing beats the real thing and your turtles will love the authentic smells and the rustle of leaves as they move around in them.

Plants will also provide extra cover and some interesting places to explore around making them a very welcome addition to the vivarium and adding to your turtles overall happiness.

Water

Turtles really do like having a good soak. They are turtles after all! So it's very important to have a large water bowl that's at least an inch deep so that they can at least half submerge themselves if they want to. This is a minimum and we recommend a sloped bathing area if possible with enough water to completely submerge should they like to.

If you are breeding your box turtles or if you are buying a small one, you have to be very careful with your water level. Turtles can drown if they get stuck in the bowl and the water level is too deep. So if this is the case, you might want to start off with something shallow and easy to get out of for the little guys.

You can use any type of shallow bowl for this task really. Most of the specialist reptile water bowls aren't big enough for the turtles to really have a good soak as they are mainly intended for drinking purposes. Just try and find one with edges that will make it easy for your turtles to get in and out, as they aren't the most agile of creates to say the least.

The other option is to use something with vertical sides or something that is deeper and harder for them to get out, but to counter this, add some rocks or wood at the sides so that they can easily get in and out. This is a great way of getting the water deep enough that they can have a good swim, but also making sure they can get safely back to dry land any time they want.

The other option, if you are keeping your turtles outside like we recommend, is to dig them a mini turtle pond. All you need is a small section of pond liner and some sand. Simply dig a hole that's the correct size, shape and depth then line it with sand, lay the pond liner over the top and fill with water. You can tidy up the edges with some rocks and add a log or a connected section of sticks to make climbing out of the water as easy as possible.

Lighting and Heating

If you are keeping your turtles outdoors then the sun should do all of the lighting for you, making your life much easier. This is the ideal choice and what we would definitely recommend.

In some colder regions and in the colder months, it's a good idea to offer your turtles some form of artificial heating in an outdoor enclosure. A heat lamp in the windproof area we discussed earlier would be ideal for use in colder weather.

If you have to keep your turtles indoors for some reason, then you don't want to go overboard with the heat. Here is a guide to temperate for an indoor vivarium:

- Daytime Temperature: 72F

- Basking Spot - 85F

- Nighttime Temperature: 65F

An all-round the vivarium temperature of about 72F (22C) is ideal. You should also provide a basking area with a low intensity heat source if they do want to warm themselves up a bit.

If you are keeping your box turtles indoors, you are going to need to provide some form of artificial sunlight as they won't be getting much, if any at all. Without sunlight, your turtles will not be able to process calcium. Calcium deficiency is a huge problem in captive box turtles, so this really does need to be addressed. If they cannot process calcium properly they will be highly susceptible to Metabolic Bone Disease, abnormal shell growth and deformities.

UVB Lighting is the best way to provide artificial sunlight for your box turtles. This lighting should be made available for at least 10 hours a day and switched off every night. To automate this, you can simply get a timer switch and set the on-off times.

UVB lamps such as the PowerSun are fantastic because they offer UVB lighting and a heat source for your basking spot in one convenient package. Combine with the Reptile Lamp Stand and the Deep Dome Lamp Fixture and you have a fantastic heat and light source.

Let your turtles have access to natural sunshine whenever possible, and always remember to provide a shaded area where they can retreat from the heat if needed.

Monitoring

You will need a way of monitoring the heat and humidity of your indoor vivarium to ensure that optimal conditions are being met. A very cost effective item that does the job is the Analog Dual Thermometer and Humidity Gauge.

Although if you want to get really specific and read the temperature of different areas of the vivarium, such as the hides and the basking spots (highly recommended), then you're going to need to use some more advanced pieces of kit.

A great probe is the Exo Terra Digital Combination Thermometer/ Hygrometer. You can use one of these to read the temperature and humidity of the vivarium and another to check the temperate of the basking spot.

Another great and even more gadget like option for taking heat readings is the Zoo Med ReptiTemp. This is an infrared, point and click thermometer can read temperatures at a distance. A great piece of technology and very handy to read temperate anywhere in the vivarium at the click of a button.

FEEDING AND DIET

Insects

If you have a young box turtle, or if you are breeding box turtles, you will definitely want to prove them with a readily available supply of insects to eat.

As I mentioned earlier in the book, young box turtles will eat mostly insects when they are growing because of the protein needed to develop. However, unlike a lot of other reptiles that should eat a mainly herbivorous diet, box turtles can eat insects throughout their whole lives without any real issues arising.

The best and easiest thing to feed your box turtle, insect-wise are things like snails, slugs, grasshoppers, earthworms, crickets, wax worms, cicadas, sow bugs and mealworms. Box turtles absolutely love mealworms so you shouldn't have any problems getting them to start feeding on meal worms right away.

Sometimes box turtles do take a little while to get settled in to their new surroundings and feeling comfortable, so sometimes they won't eat right away. If this does happen, just give it some time and keep trying each day and within a week you should have some success.

Some people also feed low-fat dog food with great success. Just make sure you only feed the low-fat varieties and not high-fat cat foods as too much fat can lead to Steatitis or fatty liver issues.

Vegetables, Salad and Fruits

As with most reptiles, you can feed box turtles a wide variety of greens and vegetables. However, you should definitely avoid feeding them broccoli and spinach as both of these foods will block calcium absorption. We recommend feeding strawberries, apple, banana, mushrooms, pear and green-leafed vegetables.

Most box turtles will eat the salad and vegetables willingly, however some are bit more picky. They may be unwilling to break their early eating habits and will only really want to eat insects.

I great tip to get your box turtles eating vegetables is to trick them into thinking they are eating a mealworm. Turtles aren't the brightest animals in the world so it's actually pretty easy to do this. All you need to do is cut some vegetables into meal worm sized strips (this works particularly well with apple).

Next, hold a mealworm in your hand and show it to your turtle. When the meal worm starts wriggling about in front of it, your turtle should open its mouth ready to eat, at this point you simply have the mealworm shaped strip of apple in your other hand and you put it up to its mouth. It will bite without thinking twice and they will usually eat the whole strip right away.

Sometimes, when the turtle has noticed that it's not moving, it will stop eating. This is when you need to re-engage the sneaky tactics and wriggle it with your fingers. As soon as they see it moving they should have another bite.

Try changing things up and using different vegetables. If you keep doing this, before long your turtle will be used to eating vegetables and will eat them willingly without having to go through the trickery process each time.

How Much Should You Feed?

A quick and easy rule for knowing how much you should feed your turtle is that you should feed the same amount of food as the size of their head. So try to imagine how much food would fit in their head if it was hollow! That's roughly how much they should be eating each day.

This is due to some pretty simple logic. A turtles head is about the same size as its stomach, so there you have it!

Supplements

Vitamin supplements are a great idea to keep your box turtles in the best health possible and ensure they have all of the vitamins and nutrients that they require.

Vitamin-A deficiency and calcium deficiency are both common problems in box turtles. Some kind of multi-vitamin and a calcium supplement added to the turtles food a couple of times a week will help a great deal to help prevent these issues from arising.

You can find specialist supplements online and in specialist pet stores without too much difficulty. There are some brands that actually provide specialist box turtle supplement powders which work great. All you do is simply sprinkle the recommended amount over their food.

As I mentioned, box turtles require a good amount of vitamin-A in their diet. Although the supplement powder will most probably contain a good amount of vitamin A, a great way to make sure they are getting enough is to simply add a light drizzle of cod liver oil to their food a couple of times a week. Don't worry about giving them slightly too much, it's better than them not getting enough and it would be very hard to make them sick by overdosing them on it.

A Note on Outdoor Enclosures

Something we felt necessary to add to this feeding section is that, in an outdoor enclosure, insects will more than likely come passing through regularly. This will give your turtles a readily available supply of food that they can hunt in a very natural way.

This is fantastic for your turtles as it will give them a varied diet and make things a bit more enjoyable for them as they will get to hunt in a more natural and instinctive way. For adult turtles, these random insects will probably provide all of the protein they need. So you can just feed them their vegetables along with their supplements and not have to worry too much about feeding them meal worms and other insects.

Also when you water the enclosure to keep the humidity up, this will draw worms up to the surface and attract slugs, which the turtles will snap up readily.

Fasting

Box turtles have a quite worrying trait. They will sometimes decide not to eat for extended periods of time for no apparent reason. If you notice that you have a box turtle that hasn't eaten for over a week, it's best to seek advice from a local veterinarian, but it's usually nothing to worry about and they will start eating again of their own accord.

This fasting could possibly be attributed to being too cold. The turtles bodies and metabolism will slow down as they get colder and so they will eat less. This is perfectly normal as the weather starts to get cold, however if you have indoor turtles, check your vivarium temperatures to make sure everything is in order.

BREEDING

Sexing

The first thing you're going to need to know if you want to breed your box turtle is how to tell the gender. It's fairly easy with box turtles luckily.

The males will usually have red eyes and the females will have brown eyes. It really is that simple, so anyone can easily identify the gender of most box turtles in seconds without even having to handle them.

The most reliable way to tell male from female however is to pick them up and examine their plastron (underbody shell). Males will have a concave area under the hinge. Another giveaway is the fact that males have longer tails than the females.

Breeding Conditions

Box turtles tend to mate immediately following or during rain because of the high humidity levels needed for the eggs to survive. They also tend to breed starting in the spring and going right through into autumn.

Mating Rituals and Process

Two mating box turtles are fascinating to watch. Yes I am aware how strange that sounds! There are differences in the exact process between different species. Most will circle, bite and push each other about before mounting. Some may also pulsate their throats at different stages throughout the ritual.

The important part however is pretty much the same across the board. This is where the males concave plastron comes in to play. It enables him to fit better against the females shell and get into the proper position. After the male has inseminated the female, he may fall off backwards in a comical fashion. This however isn't funny for the males, who sometimes get stuck on their backs. This can result in getting stuck for a long time and eventually lead to death for the unfortunate male. If this happens, give him a helping hand.

Eggs

Box turtle eggs are soft shelled and oblong shaped. They are generally very small in size at about 2–4 cm long. Clutch sizes vary depending on many factors and can range anywhere from just 1 egg up to 6 or 7.

Northern box turtles tend to produce a larger amount of eggs per breeding cycle, whereas southern varieties of box turtle have more cycles per year. Female box turtles can actually lay fertile eggs for up to about four years after being inseminated by just one male.

Prior to laying their eggs, the females will dig a nest in the soil using their hind legs. She will then ley her eggs before covering the nest over to help keep in the humidity and maintain a constant temperature. The same female can lays several clutches in a single year.

Box turtle eggs require a high level of humidity. If conditions are too dry, the eggs can actually dehydrate and collapse. A humidity level of over 80% is highly recommended, at a temperature of about 80F. If conditions are right, your first box turtle hatchlings will emerge from the eggs in roughly 70-80 days.

There have been reports that suggest box turtle eggs which are incubated at temperatures as low as 75F produce more males and those incubated at temperatures of about as 85F produce more females. At about 80F you should get a nice mix.

Another tip is to disturb the eggs as little as possible. Unlike bird eggs, you should not turn box turtle eggs. This can actually do a lot of damage and even kill the embryo. You can very carefully remove them and place them in an incubator in order to simulate the best conditions possible, just don't roll them and be as gentle as possible when digging them up and moving them.

Hatchling Care

When the hatchlings first emerge, they may take some time to fully exit the shell. This is normal and some may even take a couple of days to fully emerge. You should not rush or try to coax them out as they will still have the yolk sack attached to their underside. This is easily damaged and ruptured which can easily prove fatal. The yolk sack will be quickly absorbed and they will be far safer to handle in just one or two days.

This yolk sack can sustain the hatchlings for at least a few weeks, so if they don't want to feed for a while, that's perfectly normal, just keep trying every day and eventually they will start to want to feed on insects.

They will also want to hide almost all of the time. This is probably due to the fact that in the wild they are too small to properly defend themselves, so they need to keep out of sight of predators as much as possible. So make sure they have plenty of hiding spots available to them.

The juvenile box turtles should be kept separate from the adults until they are much older. The reason for this is because, if the adults have any kind of parasitic infection, this can be passed on to the weaker juveniles, which can prove to be fatal.

Hatchlings and young box turtles are also very sensitive to environmental and dietary factors. You must ensure their living conditions and dietary requirements are as optimal as possible to guarantee a high success rate.

HIBERNATION

As the weather gets colder you will notice that your box turtles will eat less and less as time goes on. They will also move about less and generally be less active.

They may even hide away for days at a time. This could be in a hide that you have provided for them, but they will probably also begin to dig holes in the ground and stay there for extended periods of time. They may well decide to make these holes their home for the winter.

We suggest adding extra dry leaves to the enclosure during this time, as this can act as an extra layer of insulation from the frost. If you have a mesh top to your enclosure, it is also a good idea to lay a sheet of wood or plastic over the top to prevent too much rain or snow getting in. It's also a great idea to cover the enclosure with something like old carpet, weighed down with some rocks or bricks.

If you have any sick or underweight turtles, it is very important that you keep them inside over the winter. Only healthy animals will survive hibernation, so this is of vital importance.

Other than that, just let them get on with it! In the wild they have to deal with hibernation and cold conditions, so as long as you don't live in a particularly cold part of the world and you cover the enclosure with carpet and add the dry leaves for insulation, they should be fine.

DISEASES AND ILLNESS

Box turtles are generally very hardy animals when kept outside and in well fed, so you shouldn't run into too many issues.

A lot of health issues that affect box turtles are generally due to mistakes made by their owners, often as a result of poor advice. Also box turtles have been found to suffer far more health issues when kept in a vivarium indoors, this is also probably due to the increased chance of human error.

In this chapter we are going to go over some of the common mistakes and misconceptions that cause illness in box turtles, along with some information on the common illnesses.

Environment

It's vital to ensure that your turtles are not exposed to high heat levels or dry conditions. While it's true that box turtles are found in temperate regions in the wild, they are not found in extremely hot, tropical areas. Many owners do tend to treat box turtles like a tropical reptile, so it's important to remember that they are not. So excessive heat and dryness is not good for them at all. If exposed to excessive heat, box turtles can suffer from metabolic stress and kidney failure.

Wild Food

As I mentioned, when box turtles are kept in an outdoor enclosure, they will be presented with a range of insects that they will more than happily feed on. The only problem with this is when the insects they are eating have come into contact with harmful chemicals.

You should never use any kind of pesticides in your garden if you are keeping box turtles in an outdoor enclosure. Something that is especially problematic is slug pellets, as box turtles love to eat slugs and snails. This can be extremely hazardous so really do be careful with this.

Swollen and Closed Eyes

Eye problems in box turtles are generally caused by low humidity, but can also be caused by dirty drinking and bathing water. Eye issues will cause your box turtle to stop eating, sometimes completely depending on the severity of the problem.

The treatment for this condition is generally antibiotics, which you can get from your vet. This will generally clear the issue easily enough.

Ear Abscesses

This problem is also caused by low humidity and is probably one of the most common issues that you are likely to run into.

The treatment for ear abscesses is far more unpleasant this time round unfortunately. If your turtle does indeed have an ear abscess, it will need to be lanced by a vet. This will also require draining and aftercare from a trained professional.

Pneumonia

Pneumonia in turtles is a very serious problem and will require immediate attention from a veterinarian. If your turtle has pneumonia, their neck and head movements may become strained, they will become lethargic and they may produce excess mucus.

Sore Skin

Skin conditions are usually caused by either a vitamin-A deficiency or dirty living conditions. It can also be a sign that your turtle may have a liver issue. If you notice that your turtle has a skin condition, seek advice from a vet right away.

Parasites

Due to the fact that box turtles feed on insects, they are prone to contracting parasites. The most common parasites are various types of worms. A vet an examine a stool sample to determine if an animal has a parasitic infection and provide the appropriate treatment.

Things to Look Out For

- Changes in eating or behavior for more over 2 weeks at a time (unless hibernating)
- Strange or discolored areas on the shell or skin
- Dry or flaky shell and skin
- Mucus and any other discharge from the nose
- Swelling and lumps (especially over the ear)
- Foam and any kind of discharge from the turtles mouth

Choosing a Vet

We realize that you may not always have the luxury of choosing a vet, especially if you need one out of hours, but you should choose one very carefully if you can.

The reason we suggest this is because most vets are used to only treating cats and dogs. A good reptile vet is hard to come by, but if you find one that is highly experienced in treating and dealing with reptiles, this is usually because they chose to learn more about it of their own accord. So you can be sure that these vets can be trusted to look after your sick animals.

FINAL THOUGHTS

Well that about wraps it up for this book! I hope you gained some useful information.

We have plenty of other books out about loads of topics surrounding Pet Care and we put our new books up for free trials every now and again. You can view all of our books by simply searching for "Pet Care Expert" on Amazon.

Thanks so much for taking an interest in our books and I hope to speak to you all again very soon!

CPSIA information can be obtained
at www.ICGtesting.com
Printed in the USA
BVOW06s1616281117
501475BV00024B/91/P

9 781517 152864